Sunita and the V

by Kaye Um...
illustrated by Tom Clayton

THE CAST

SUNITA

RAVI

BILLY

MRS GOHILL
(Ravi and Sunita's mum)

MRS STEEL
(Billy's mum)

Scene 1

The Summer Fair at school. Sunita has her face painted. She is showing her mum, who is on the clothes stall.

SUNITA   Look, Mummy. I'm Bad Bert.

MRS GOHILL   Lovely, Sunita.
                 Do you want that scarf, sir? Only ten pence.

A customer comes to the stall.

SUNITA   Can I have some more money?

MRS GOHILL   Not now.
                 Thank you, sir.

SUNITA   But I want to buy things.

MRS GOHILL   No, Sunita. No more.

SUNITA   Why not?

Clothes
+
Shoes

Old Shoes

MRS GOHILL Because you have already had your pocket money.

SUNITA Auntie sent me five pounds. Can I have that?

MRS GOHILL No. Five pounds is a lot to carry around.

SUNITA Please, Mummy.

MRS GOHILL Oh dear. All right. But don't spend it all. And don't lose it.

Mum gives Sunita five pounds.

SUNITA Hooray! I'm rich!

Exit Sunita.

5

MRS GOHILL Ravi!

Enter Ravi.

RAVI Yes, Mum?

MRS GOHILL Your sister has five pounds. Will you keep an eye on her?

RAVI Oh, Mum! Must I? I want to help Billy with the Wishing Well.

MRS GOHILL Please, Ravi. I don't trust her with all that money.

RAVI Oh, all right.

MRS GOHILL Good boy. Don't let her spend it all on silly things.

Exit Ravi.

7

Scene 2

Sunita is standing before the toy stall. She has a lot of toys in her arms.

Enter Ravi.

RAVI Sunita! What are you doing?

SUNITA Buying toys. Look! A teddy, a doll, and a poor old monkey.

RAVI You don't need more toys. You have lots of toys at home.

SUNITA I want these too. Oh, look! A lovely hat!

Exit Sunita.

RAVI Sunita! Come back!

He runs after her.

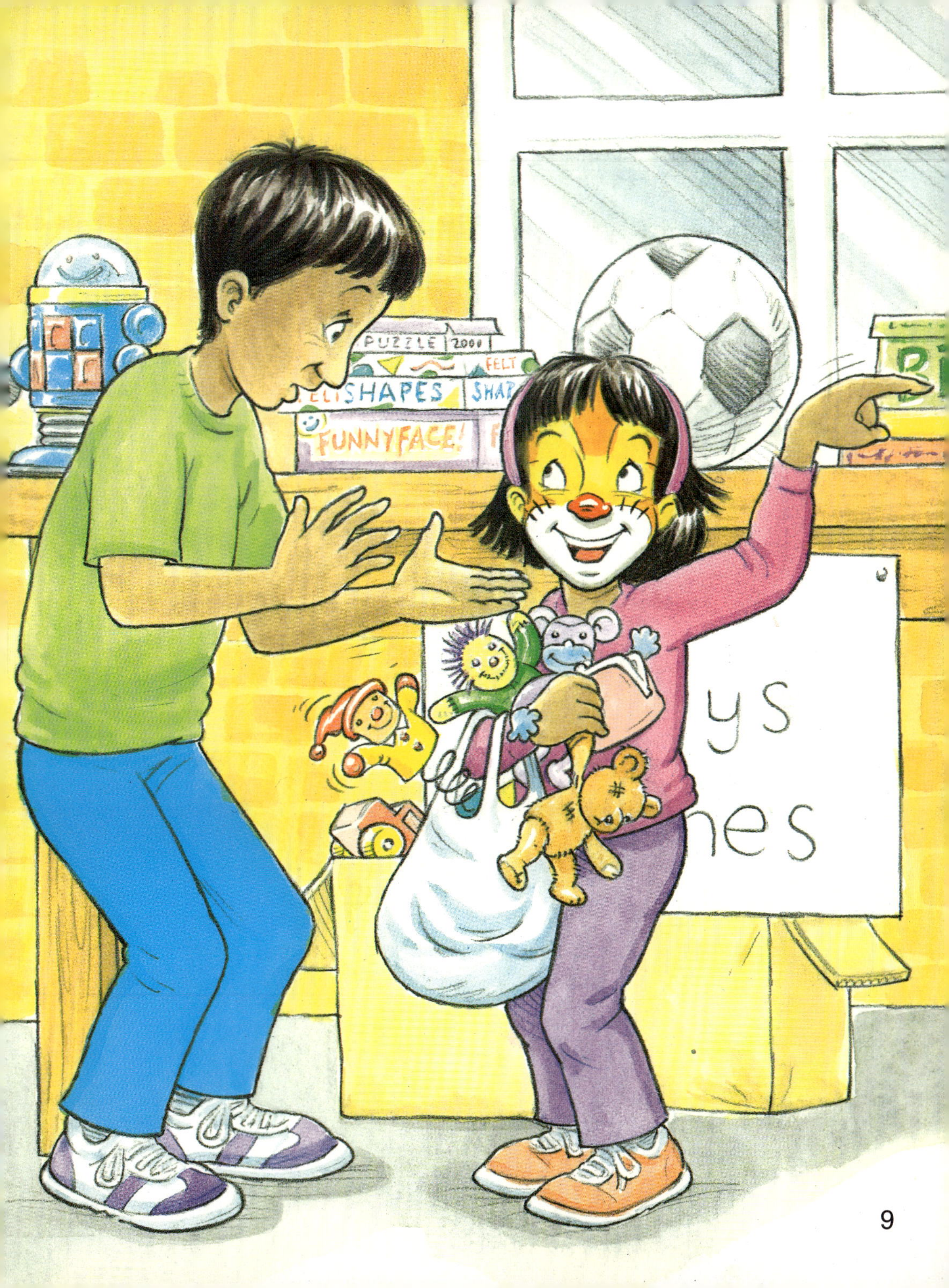
PUZZLE
2000
FELT
SHAPES
FUNNYFACE!

Scene 3

Sunita at the junk stall. She has bought a hat, a china owl and a clock.

Enter Ravi.

RAVI	**Now** what have you got?
SUNITA	Some good things.
RAVI	Rubbish, you mean.
SUNITA	It's not rubbish.
RAVI	Why do you want a clock? You can't tell the time yet.
SUNITA	I can. I like it.
RAVI	It's broken. It doesn't go.
SUNITA	I still like it. Go away, Ravi.

bric-a-brac

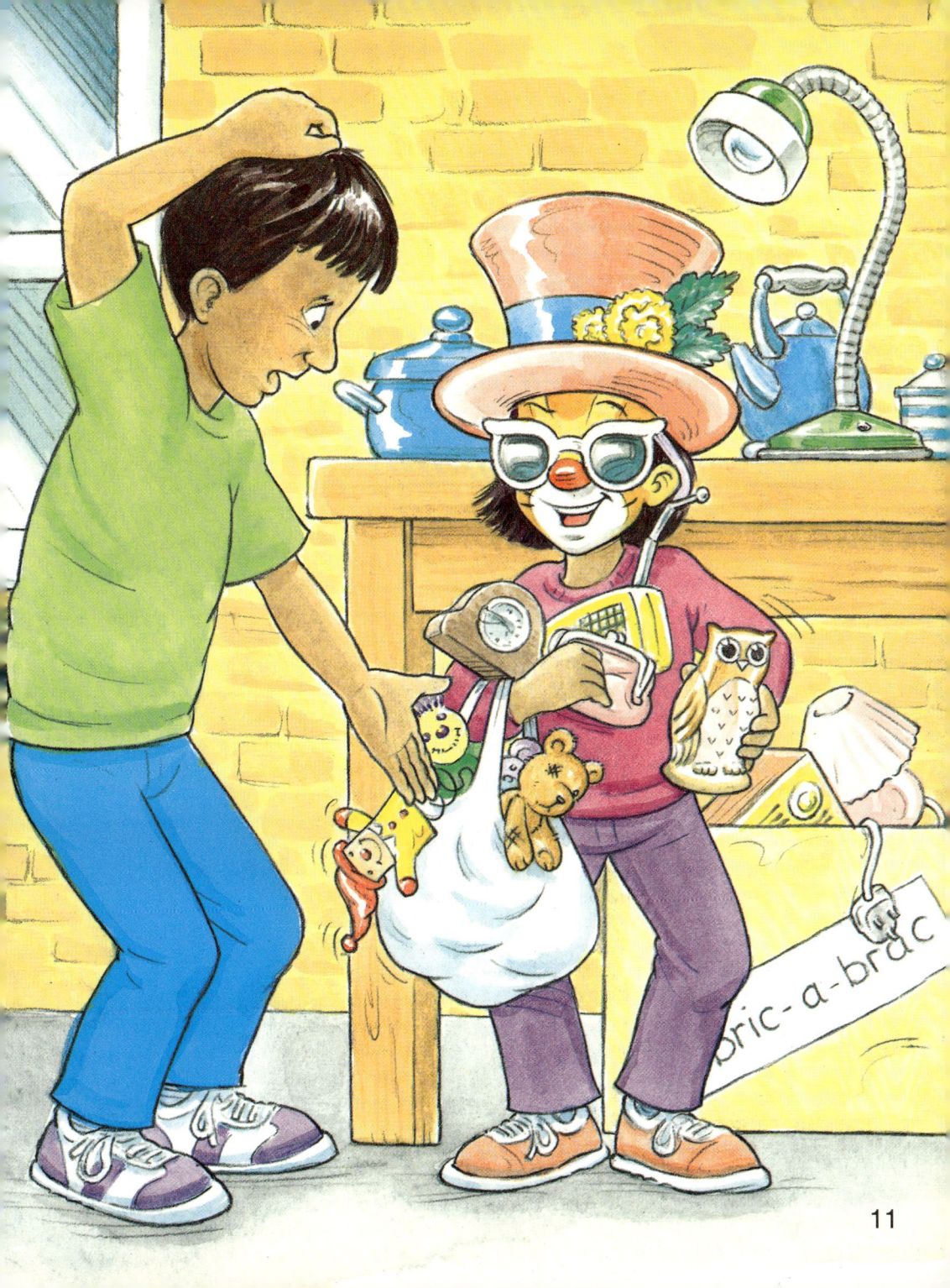

RAVI You are spending all your money on silly things.

SUNITA They are not silly.

RAVI They are. Mum will be cross.

SUNITA Don't be bossy. Ooh! Candy floss!

Sunita points off stage and exits.

Mrs Steel enters.

MRS STEEL Ah! There you are, Ravi.

RAVI Hello, Mrs Steel.

MRS STEEL Billy wants you to help him with the Wishing Well.

RAVI Yes. But first I must stop Sunita spending all her money.

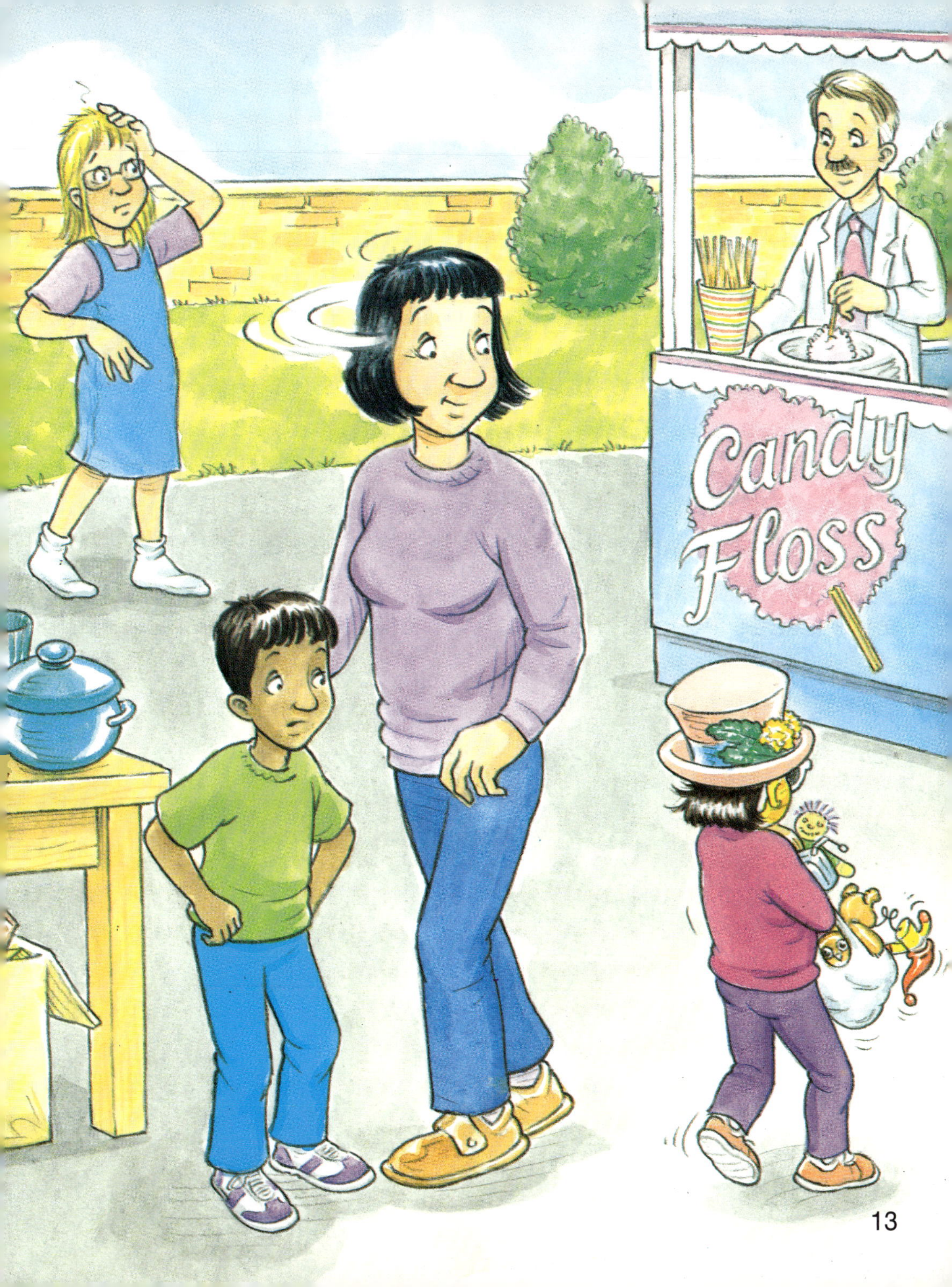
Candy Floss

MRS STEEL How much does she have?

RAVI She started with five pounds.

MRS STEEL That's a lot.

RAVI It's her birthday money. But she's spending it all on silly things.

Mrs Steel looks off stage.

MRS STEEL You had better hurry up. She is at the Candy Floss Stall.

RAVI Oh, dear. I can't stop her.

MRS STEEL And now she is going to the Lucky Dip.

RAVI Oh, no!

Exit Ravi.

15

Scene 4

Sunita has just had a go at the Lucky Dip. She is eating a stick of candy floss.

Enter Ravi.

SUNITA Look. I got a present from the Lucky Dip. A rubber spider.

RAVI So I see.

SUNITA I got some candy floss too.

RAVI Please stop spending, Sunita.

SUNITA Now. What shall I buy next? Ooh, look! Old comics! Yes!

Exit Sunita, to the comic stall.

RAVI I give up.

LUCKY DIP!

Scene 5

The Wishing Well. Billy is in charge.

Enter Ravi.

BILLY   Hello, Ravi. Where have you been?

RAVI   Don't ask. How are you doing?

BILLY   Fine. It's fun doing this.

Enter Sunita, with all her things and a big ice cream.

SUNITA   Hello, Billy.

BILLY   Hello, Sunita. Do you want to throw a coin in the Wishing Well?

SUNITA   Ooh, yes!

RAVI   NO!

He is too late. Sunita throws in her last pound coin.

BILLY   Hey! That was a **pound**!

Ye Olde
Wishing Well

Throw a coin
Make a Wish!

RAVI   Sunita! How **could** you?

SUNITA   Where is my prize?

BILLY   There is no prize. You just make a wish.

RAVI   You have wasted five pounds. What will Mum say?

Sunita starts to cry.

BILLY   Come on. Don't cry.

SUNITA   I feel sick. Boo hoo hoo!

RAVI   I did try to stop you.

SUNITA   I know. I'm sorry. Boo hoo!

Sunita hides her face and cries.

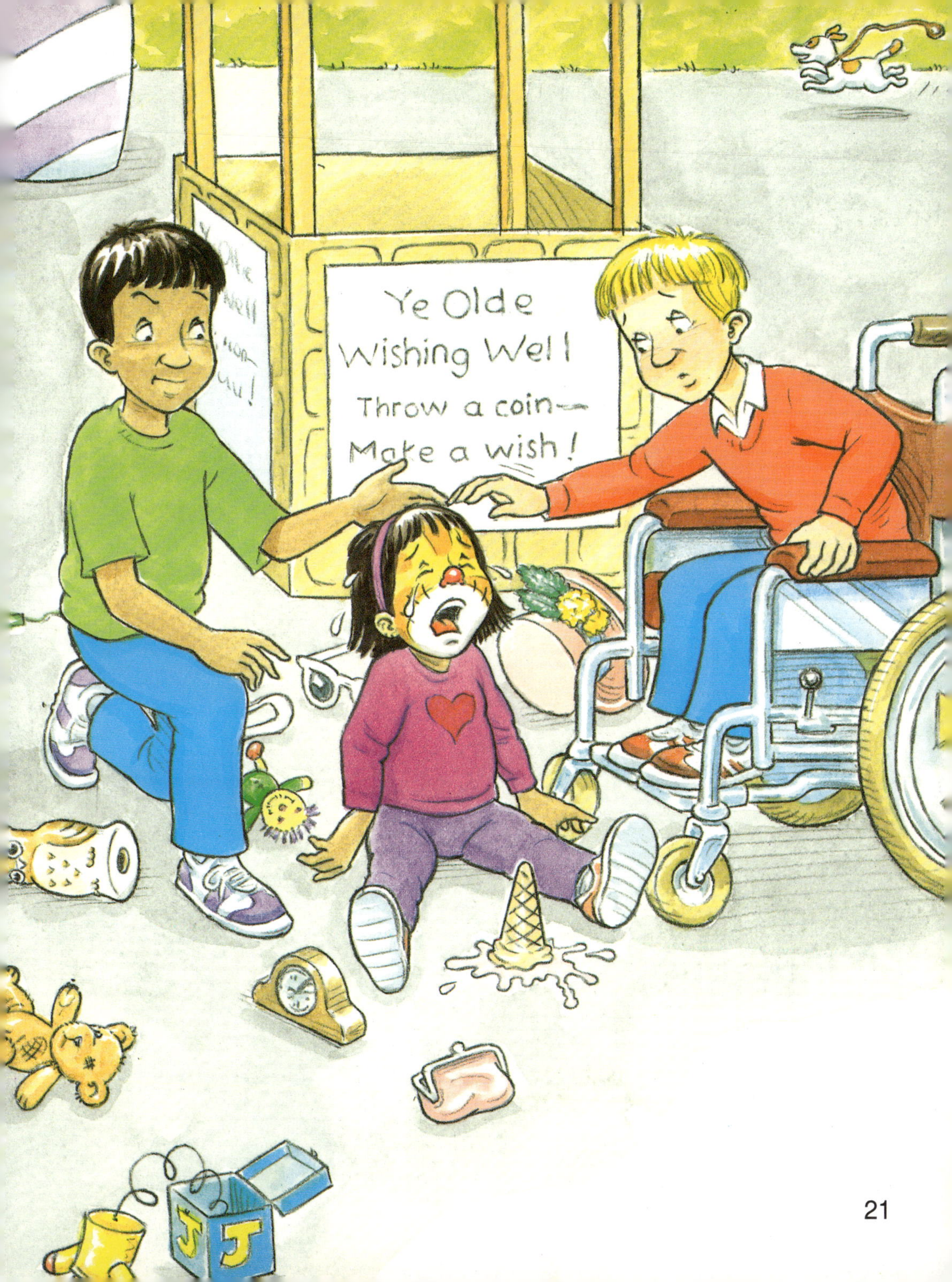
Ye Olde
Wishing Well
Throw a coin—
Make a wish!

BILLY   Cheer up, Sunita. Make a wish.

SUNITA   No. Oh, Ravi! I **wish** I had all my money back!

BILLY   Your wish is my command! Here.

Billy takes five pounds from his pocket and gives it to Sunita.

RAVI   What are you doing?

BILLY   Granting her wish.

SUNITA   Ooh. Magic! Thank you, Billy.

RAVI   Now, go back to Mum!

SUNITA   I will.

Exit Sunita.

RAVI   Thanks, Billy. That was kind.

23

BILLY Any time.

RAVI I'll pay you back.

Enter Mrs Steel.

MRS STEEL Ravi! I have just seen Sunita at the plant stall.

RAVI Oh no. What's she buying **now**?

MRS STEEL A present for Billy, she said.

RAVI Aaargh!

BILLY Quick! Stop her!

They both exit in a hurry.

THE END